# Let's Talk About
# BEING WASTEFUL

# Let's Talk About
# BEING WASTEFUL
## By JOY BERRY

*Illustrated by John Costanza*

*Edited by Kate Dickey*

*Designed by Abigail Johnston*

GROLIER ENTERPRISES CORP.

Let's talk about BEING WASTEFUL.

You are being wasteful when you use more of something than you need.

You are being wasteful when you damage or destroy something.

It may be impossible to replace the things you waste.

You may run out of something you need.

You must not be wasteful so that you will have what you need.

There are many things that help you to survive and grow. You need
- food
- water
- clothes
- gas
- electricity
- gasoline
- supplies
- money

You need *food* to help keep your body alive and well. Try not to waste it.

- Do not take more food than you can eat.
- Eat whatever food you take.
- Do not play with your food.

You need *water* to drink. You need it to help keep your body clean. Try not to waste it.

- Do not let water run unless you are using it.
- Do not use more water than you actually need.
- Turn the water faucet off completely after you are finished using it. Do not leave it dripping.

You need *clothes* to protect your body and help keep it warm. Try not to waste them.

- Avoid getting your clothes dirty.
  Dirt can ruin them. Clothes that must be cleaned often wear out faster.
- Do not damage your clothes.
- Do not lose your clothes.

You need *gas, electricity,* or *other kinds of fuel.* These things help provide light so that you can see. They help keep the temperature in your home comfortable. They run the appliances you and your family use. Try not to waste fuel.

- Turn the lights off in rooms that no one is using.
- Do not turn on the heater or air conditioner unless you have permission to do so.
- Turn off any appliance that is not being used.

You need *gasoline*. It helps move the cars and buses that take you where you need to go. Try not to waste it.

- Ask someone to drive you only when it is necessary.
- Whenever possible, walk or ride a bike.

You need *supplies* like pencils, paper, toilet paper, soap, shampoo, and bandaids. Try not to waste these things.

Do not use more of anything than you actually need.

You need *money*. Money helps you buy the things you need and want. Try not to waste it.

- Do not buy things that you are not going to use.
- Buy the things you need before you buy the things you want.
- Take care of your money. Do not lose it.

Being wasteful is not good for you or others.

Wastefulness can use up the valuable resources that you need to survive and grow.

Avoid being wasteful.

You must take care of the things around you
so that you will have what you need.